# Celebrating
# a Celtic Halloween

GWASG CARREG GWALCH

First published: September 2005
© text: Gwasg Carreg Gwalch 2005
© poems: the poets 2005
© illustrations/photographs: the illustrators/photographers 2005

ISBN: 0-86381-938-9

Published by Gwasg Carreg Gwalch,
12 Iard yr Orsaf, Llanrwst,
Dyffryn Conwy,
Wales LL26 0EH
phone 01492642031
fax 01492641502
e-mail llyfrau@carreg-gwalch.co.uk
website www.carreg-gwalch.co.uk

**Editor**
Gordon Jones

**Photographs**
Keith Morris: pp cover, 6, 16 top, 17, 28-29, 54-55
Myrddin ap Dafydd: pp 11, 14, 15, 16 bottom, 28-29,
Marian Delyth: pp 27, 31, 48-49, 50, 52, 58-59

**Original Welsh text**
Myrddin ap Dafydd
Emily Huws
Gordon Jones

**English text**
Siân Lewis
Gwyn Morgan
Geraint Løvgreen

**Illustrations**
James Field: pp 7-9, 22-24, 26, 32, 33 bottom, 34
Graham Howells: pp 10-13, 30, 33 top, 35, 38, 40-41
Robin Lawrie: pp 18-21, 42-44, 46-47, 55-57, 60-63
Ruth Jên: pp 36-37

**Recipes**
Jane Bailey: pp 27, 31, 53, 58-59

**Design**
Sion Ilar, The Welsh Books Council

The publishers wish to acknowledge the support of the Welsh Books Council

Printed in Belgium by Proost

# contents

# 31
## October

# Halloween

This is a date we all remember: the night when ugly old witches ride out on their broomsticks, when ghosts roam the land. This is the night when fearsome fiends, bearded beasts, menacing monsters and sinister spooks are on the loose. Watch out they don't get you!

Of course none of this is true. It's an old wives' tale – a superstition – but at one time most people believed in it. Today many children look forward to the 31st of October. It's a night of fun and laughter, of scaring people with a game of 'trick or treat' or taking part in a creepy fancy dress party. Today Halloween is a source of innocent fun, but long ago things were very different.

Who were the first to celebrate Halloween? The Americans? The English? The Greeks? The Romans? No, it was probably the Celts, the ancestors of the Welsh, who started it all a long time ago.

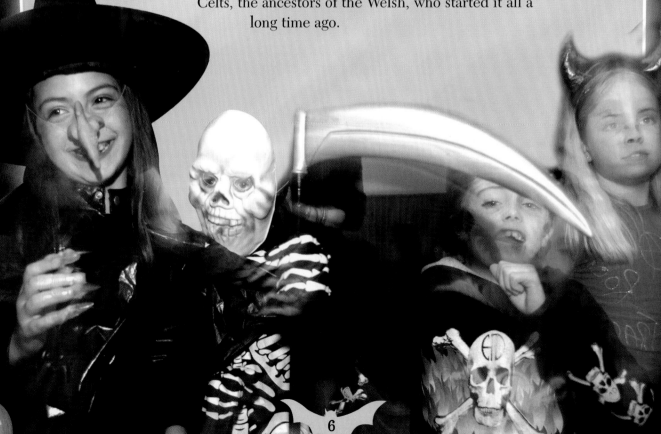

# The Celts

Thousands of years ago the Celts lived throughout the length and breadth of Europe. They were farmers and divided the year into two parts – the light summer and the dark winter. They knew that the sun made their crops grow. As autumn drew near, the sun lost its strength. The Celts believed that winter kept the sun prisoner for six months.

They were afraid they would never see the sun again. So, to make sure the sun came back, they held a festival on the 31st of October. At that time they called it the Festival of Samhain. For the Celts, winter began on the 1st of November, which was also the first day of their new year, a time when plants withered and died. Life would not return till the following summer.

During Samhain people would be sacrificed to the gods, because the Celts thought this would please them and that it would result in fine weather and a fruitful farming year. They left food out for the dead, because they also believed that ghosts returned on that night.

# The Bonfires of the Celts

During the Festival of Samhain the Celts asked the sun to come back safely the next summer. They put out all their cooking fires. Then they built huge bonfires on the hillsides and prayed that the sun would shine brightly when winter was over.

The next morning, the morning of the festival, everyone would return to the hillside, pull the burning wood embers from the ashes of the bonfires, and use them to light new fires on their hearths. They believed the new fires would bring good luck. Then they cooked huge feasts on the fires. Everyone would wear special clothes made from animal skins. They believed that the clothes, the headdresses and the frightening masks would protect them from bad luck, evil spirits and fairies.

Before the Celts became Christians the festival was known as the Day of the Dead. Later, when Christianity came to Wales, people began to celebrate All Saints' Day on the first of November – the day when the saints who have died are remembered. The Day of the Dead then became All Hallows' Eve, which means the day before the festival of 'hallows' (saints). This term then changed into Hallowe'en and eventually into Halloween.

So Halloween is a very ancient festival. It began with the Celts dressing up in animal skins on October 31st, and people have been dressing up at Halloween ever since.

To avoid being recognised and caught by the ghosts and strange creatures that roamed the land on that night, people – children in particular – used to carry turnip lanterns to light their path. That is another tradition that has survived to the present. Some would join in the celebrations by blackening their faces with soot from the big chimney. This protected them from evil spirits and brought them good luck. To avoid being recognised and snatched by the fiends, women dressed up as men and men as women. It's fun putting on strange costumes and masks and scaring other people, and this is one of the main reasons why people are still doing so after hundreds of years.

# Halloween Stories

Everyone enjoys a good story, no matter where they live. That's why millions of us watch films and soap operas on the television nowadays. Today, if we want to be entertained, all we have to do is open a book or press the switch of the telly or computer.

Long ago, people had none of these things, so they came together to tell and listen to stories, to dance and sing, especially during the long, dark, barren winter nights when they could not work outside. In the old days the Welsh called this season 'Hirlwm', which means 'a long, barren time'. Just as the stories in our books and soap operas reflect our lives, the people then told stories about their own lives – about all the things that scared and worried them and the things that made them happy.

The Celts believed that, before they came to Wales, the little people – the fairies – used to live here. These fairies had all sorts of magic powers, both good and bad. If you happened to walk into a fairy ring, you would fall under their spell and be lured into their country. Many were afraid that they, or their children, would be taken away forever by the fairies. They were also afraid that the fairies would sneak into their homes and swap a happy, contented baby for one of their own grumpy bad-tempered fairy children.

At that time too, most people were scared of witches. Witches were at their worst on Halloween, when they would ride out on their broomsticks.

All sorts of ugly, gruesome creatures roamed the land. In some areas people were scared of a huge ghostly black pig without a tail. In other areas people left the lamp burning all night to ward off evil spirits.

So on Halloween people used to come together to tell stories about all those things that scared them. Today Halloween story sessions are still popular in libraries and schools throughout the country, and in this book there are old stories about the ghosts and fairies of Wales for you to read.

# The Cropped Black Sow

Menacing monsters! Bearded beasts! Creepy creatures! Fearsome fiends!
Horrible hags! Awful apparitions! Gory ghouls –
all creeping through the shadows on Halloween!

It's Halloween,
and there's a ghost
on every post!

It's Halloween,
and monsters will be seen!

Tailless black sow
is after you now . . .
tailless black sow
will catch you – ow!

It's Halloween tonight
When ghosts give us a fright
And Jack o'Lanterns roam –
It's time to run for home.

Run, run, run homewards fast,
Tailless black sow will take the last.

Welsh people of long ago used to believe that the Cropped Black Sow ran wild through the land at the end of their bonfire celebrations. Anyone unlucky enough to be caught would be eaten.
   The Black Sow was a monster that had been set free for that one night. This was the time when farmers used to set their pigs loose in the woods to eat fallen acorns – and there's nothing worse than coming face to face with a big dark sow when you're walking through the woods in the dead of night!

# Jack-o'-Lantern

Jack-o'-Lantern was an old man who was too wicked to go to heaven. He wasn't allowed to go to hell either, because he'd played tricks on the devil. Some say he's still wandering from place to place scaring people with his lantern.

What if Jack and the other creepy creatures padded along the paths . . . to your house? Sneaked through the streets . . . to your house? Ducked through the doors, sidled up the stairs, breezed into the bedrooms . . . of your house?

You better watch out for witches! Guard against ghosts, ghouls and ghastly things! Save yourself from spooks! But how?

*To find out, turn to the next page . . .*

# Punkie Lantern

The best way to scare evil spirits is to make a Punkie (or Ghostly) Lantern for Halloween. Don't even think of being without one – seriously! And another thing: it's no good buying one. To protect your house properly, you've got to make one yourself. So, off you go! There are several vegetables you can use, but the most common are swedes and pumpkins. A pumpkin is softer than a swede and easier to handle.

## You need

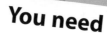

- a pumpkin
- a sharp knife
- a large metal spoon
- a dark felt pen
- a small night light candle

1. Ask an adult to help you cut off the top of the pumpkin with the sharp knife. Keep the top to use as a lid.
2. With the spoon hollow out the pumpkin, leaving a shell about 3cm thick.
3. Use the felt pen to draw eyes, a nose and a mouth on the pumpkin.
4. Ask an adult to cut out the shapes with the sharp knife.
5. Put the candle inside the pumpkin.
6. Decide on the best place for your pumpkin (it has to be safe too) and put it in position.
7. Ask an adult to light the candle and pop the lid on top.

# Bubble, Bubble

How about a mugful of witches' black brew? There's nothing better than a hot drink on a cold night.

No? You don't fancy witches' brew? Can't blame you. Goodness knows what's in it. So how about making this soup? You'll know exactly what's in this:

## Blood Broth

Well, it's red anyway …

How do you make this deliciously gory broth?

- 🎃 Easy! You already have the most important ingredient.
- 🎃 The flesh of the pumpkin, without the seeds. Please don't waste it.
- 🎃 Ask an adult to help you roast it in the oven with onions and tomatoes. Add tinned tomatoes.
- 🎃 Put them all through the blender.
- 🎃 Add some salt and pepper, and warm the broth in a saucepan.

## Seed Snacks

And what about the seeds? Wash them in water and dry with a cloth. Put them in a bowl and mix them with a little cooking oil and a pinch of salt. Then place them on a baking tray and roast them in the oven for about a quarter of an hour. Set aside to cool and then eat. They're very tasty.

## Bone Bracelet

You don't want to eat the seeds? Then don't bother roasting them. Let them dry for a day or two. Take a length of cotton. Tie a knot in the end. Thread the other end through a needle. Now thread the seeds onto the cotton to make a necklace and bracelets.
Shake the bracelet or necklace!
Listen! Can you hear them rattle?
Just like dry bones!

# We're Inviting You to a Spooky Do

It's fun pretending to be someone else – especially someone or something that looks yucky and scary. And it's better still if nobody recognises you! So for a perfect Halloween party you need to plan your make-up and fancy dress very carefully.

## The Idea

Who or what would you like to be? Read on through this book and you'll find plenty of ideas. Here are some:

Witch • Pirate • Jack-o'-Lantern • Skeleton
Dracula • Frankenstein • Wicked Wizard
Witch's cat • Green Monster • Ghost

What sort of head or clothes does your character have? Start off by making a drawing. Have a look round the shops. But don't buy too many things – making your own is fun, and it's a sure way to be different from everyone else.

## Crazy Clothes

Look around the house for interesting clothes. Simple things can be very effective. For instance a bin bag makes a good cloak.

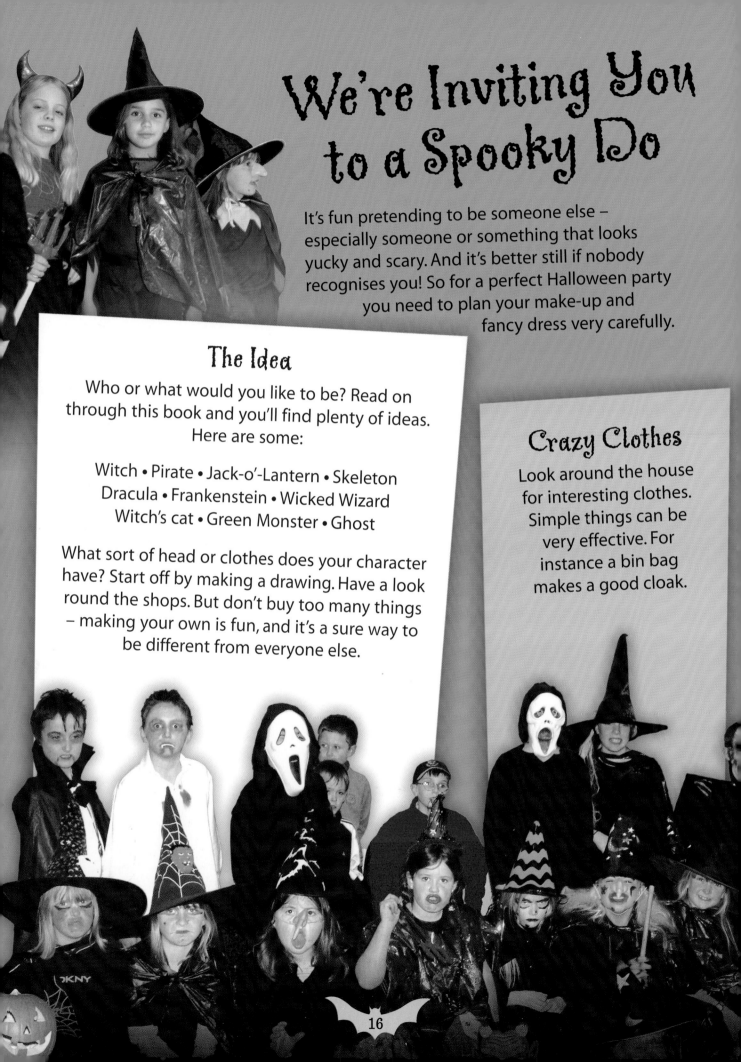

# Monster Make-up

## You need

- water-soluble face paints
- a small sponge to spread and mix colours on the face
- a fine paintbrush to draw lines
- tubes of glitter paint
- eyeliner pencil
- towels
- face flannels or disposable wipes
- soap and water
- a mirror
- hair gel

Take your time. First make a drawing on paper. It's easier if you have a friend or a parent to help you. To avoid making a mess, paint your face in the bathroom!

Paint dramatic eyebrows.

How about a scar? Blood? Hair? Sharp teeth? You could blacken one of your front teeth with an eyeliner pencil.

Add a little hair gel to make yourself scarier still!

**Warning** Make sure you're not allergic to the paint. First dab a little on your hand and wait to see if there's a reaction before using it on your face.

# Waiting for Arawn

The old name for Pembrokeshire was the Seven Regions of Dyfed and some of the best known folk tales of Wales are set there. According to a story in the Mabinogi, Pwyll, king of the Seven Regions of Dyfed, once met Arawn while out hunting in Glyn Cuch. Arawn was king of Annwn, the kingdom of the dead.

In the same area, a family living in a farmhouse in Aber-cuch had been haunted for many years by a ghost. The family was large and needed many bedrooms. Even so, one bedroom in the farmhouse was always left empty.

This was the ghost's room. In the dead of night the ghost would wail mournfully: 'Long is the day and long is the night and long is the wait for Arawn.' No one could sleep in that room. In fact the family were afraid to go inside even in bright daylight.

One cold winter's evening the family had locked their doors and were huddled around a blazing fire. Outside it was blowing up a gale, when suddenly they heard a knock on the door.

'Who's come calling at this time of night and in such stormy weather?' wondered the farmer as he got up to open the door.

There stood a weary traveller. The farmer invited him in to warm himself, and he was given a bowl of soup. It was now very late.

'You're welcome to eat your fill,' said the farmer, 'but I'm afraid I can't offer you a bed for the night, though we do have an empty room.'

'You've already been far too kind,' said the stranger. 'I don't want to take advantage of you.'

'It's not that we don't want you to stay,' said the farmer hastily, 'but we'd be afraid for your safety. There's a ghost in that room. A ghost that wails pitifully every night!'

'Oh, I'm not afraid of a ghost,' scoffed the stranger. 'I'm so tired, I dare say I won't hear a thing all night long.'

'Well, if you're quite sure . . .' said the farmer.

He led the traveller up the stairs. At the door of the bedroom, he asked him: 'You didn't tell us your name, stranger. What shall we call you?'

The traveller walked into the bedroom. 'My name is Arawn,' he said, turning to the farmer. 'Good night to you.' The bedroom door clicked shut.

That night the farmer and his wife couldn't sleep a wink, they were so worried about the poor traveller, but they didn't hear a sound from the room.

The following day, when the farmer went to knock on the door to wake their guest, he found the bedroom empty.

From that day on the ghost never wailed 'Long is the day and long is the night and long is the wait for Arawn', and the room could be used as a bedroom by the farmer and his family.

# Ghost Night

Dracula, cloaked in black,
Hiding in the chimney stack;
Bat, hanging upside-down
Casts giant shadows on the ground;
Wolf, teeth all gleaming white
Howling in the cold of night;
Bogeyman with beady eye
Through the keyhole plays I-spy;
Monster with green-coloured skin
Outside the window looking in;
Witch as ugly as the night
Through the darkness taking flight;
Skeleton with grinning jaw,
Phantoms behind every door,
Corpse-candle, evil sprite,
Skulls and daggers in the night,
And on every wooden stile
Sits a ghost with ghastly smile,
Makes me want to run a mile . . .
All these frights are to be seen
On the night of Halloween!

*Geraint Løvgreen*

## The Witching Hour

This is the witching hour
The moon is full and round,
A cold wind sweeps round corners
There's a rumble underground.
Elves, hobgoblins, witches, wizards
Appear, then fade into the night
Tonight it's darkness that will conquer,
For these creatures have no light.

*Gwyn Morgan*

20

## Scary Masks

We made scary masks in school today,
With blotches of bright paint. Look, Mother,
Isn't it ugly? It'll scare you all away –
Exactly like my little brother!

*Gwyn Morgan*

# Bonfires and Winter Homes

To Welsh people of long ago Halloween marked the halfway point of the farming year. The farming calendar was divided in two – the summer season from May Day (1 May) to Halloween and the winter season from Halloween to May Day.

In those days farm workers were employed for six months at a time, so Halloween marked the end of their period of work. After they were paid their wages, the farm hands went to the hiring fairs in search of new employment. This was another excuse for mischief-making at Halloween. After the hard work of the summer and autumn harvests, farm workers had some time to themselves and a chance to run wild. They would often steal gates on Halloween. Many a grumpy old farmer woke up the next day to find gaps between his gateposts, while many a farm hand sniggered behind his hand at the thought of it!

Farm animals were moved at Halloween and May Day. If you look at the names of farms on a map, you will see many that contain the word 'Hafod' or 'Hendre'. 'Hendre' was usually the old farmstead down in the lowlands. There the fields had more shelter from winter storms and the grass kept growing till the end of autumn. The 'Hafod' on the other hand was up in the hills and the high mountain valleys. There the grass grew well in summer but died back as Halloween drew near.

In the olden days the Welsh would move their cattle from the Hendre up to the Hafod on May Day. Throughout the summer they would tend them on the high slopes, milk them and send the butter and the cheese back down to the Hendre and to market. The fields near the Hendre were used to grow crops, and the hay and corn were harvested and stored in the barns ready for winter. Then, at Halloween, the cattle were herded back from the Hafod to the Hendre and kept on the lowlands over winter. The dairy cows were taken to the cowsheds and kept indoors until summer. So at Halloween the nature of a farmer's work would change and his most important task from then on would be keeping the animals fed.

What's it like in your classroom at this time of year? Are there a lot of coughs and colds that spread from one child to another? That often happens when summer, the long holidays and all those hours spent in the fresh air come to an end.

The same was true for cattle. The sweet grass and fresh mountain air would make their coats shine, but once they returned to the lowlands and were herded together in small fields in damp, foggy weather, they risked catching all kinds of diseases.

This was another reason why farmers built Halloween bonfires. Hedges were trimmed, dead growth cut down and gathered, old brambles and ferns and late-season gorse scraped into heaps and burnt. The fire killed germs – and, of course, was also also a good excuse for Halloween fun and games.

On Halloween every fire in every Hendre was put out and one huge bonfire lit in each neighbourhood. Then a burning ember was carried from the bonfire to light a new fire in the hearth of every Hendre. That fire was kept alight all winter by burning peat or wood that had been gathered throughout the summer and stacked near the house.

When there was nothing left of the Halloween bonfire but a heap of glowing ashes, the cattle that had been brought down from the Hafod were driven through the hot embers. People in the old days firmly believed that this would kill any germs and keep the herd healthy throughout the winter.

# The Cleansing Fire

Can you hear the hooves approaching
shuddering the withered sedge?
Can you hear the constant lowing
as they shove through purple hedge?

Can you see the summer shining
just before the dark days fall?
And the cattle all stampeding
as the herdsmen shout and call?

Can you see the red dust rising
as the hooves tramp on their way?
And the cut-back gorse and bracken
turning black from day to day?

Can you see the feet move faster,
in the fire-glow, bold and bright?
And the dying waves of summer
in the clean sweet-scented night?

*Geraint Løvgreen*

# Fascinating Facts

## Bonfire potatoes

Today there are many different foods and titbits we associate with Halloween. Feasting was important in the old days too. One traditional treat was jacket potatoes. Potatoes were stuck into the hot ashes and embers to cook, then everyone would have fun digging them out with a stick or a pitchfork and eating them.

## Apples and apple fruit

The apple is very important in Celtic history. When King Arthur was injured in the battle of Camlan, he was taken to Afallon – or Avalon, the isle of apples – to recuperate. The apple is associated with health, youth and the fruitfulness of the earth.

When new kinds of fruit came to Wales, the old people always called them apples, because to them 'apple' meant 'fruit'. When the orange first arrived, they called it 'orange apple' and a lemon was a 'yellow apple'. A tomato was known as a 'love apple'! We still use the word 'pineapple' and it is interesting that in France (the old land of the Celts) potatoes are known as *pommes de terre* and *avaloú douar* in Breton, or 'earth apples'.

## Dirty blackberries

Do you go out picking blackberries after Halloween? Of course not – by then they taste sour and horrible! Yet there are always some berries clinging to the brambles even at the end of October. According to superstition the wicked goblins and fairies spit on the blackberries on Halloween, so no one touches the dirty fruit afterwards. This is another good reason for clearing away the brambles and making a bonfire.

## Lucky stones

This is a game that young people played as they danced and celebrated around the bonfire. They each chose a stone, marked it and threw it into the flames. The next morning, after the fire had died down, they went to look for their stones. If they found their own stone, it would be their lucky stone for the rest of the year.

# Pomona's Apples

When the Romans came to Wales many years ago, they brought their customs with them.

For them autumn was a very important season. Every year, on the 31st of October, they held a festival to remember their dead relatives and also to honour the Roman goddess of trees and fruit – Pomona.

What is the most common autumn-ripening fruit? The apple, of course. So the Romans would make offerings of apples, nuts and other fruit to the goddess Pomona to thank her for the harvest. To mark these celebrations they had a great feast, ran races and played games.

Since then apples have been an important part of Halloween celebrations. Halloween was even known to some people as Apple and Candle Night.

# Toffee Apples

This is one of the most delicious Halloween foods – and one of the easiest to prepare.

**IMPORTANT** The toffee can get very hot, so always ask an adult for help.

## You need

- 🎃 6 apples, washed and dried
- 🎃 6 wooden sticks

## For the toffee

- 🎃 175g soft brown sugar
- 🎃 25g butter
- 🎃 50g golden syrup
- 🎃 ½ teaspoon lemon juice
- 🎃 6 tablespoons water
- 🎃 a saucepan with a heavy base
- 🎃 a wooden spoon
- 🎃 a bowl of cold water
- 🎃 greaseproof paper

**1** Remove the apple stalks and push a stick firmly into each apple.

**2** Put all the toffee ingredients in the saucepan. Heat gently and keep stirring with the wooden spoon until everything has dissolved.

**3** Turn up the heat and boil the mixture rapidly. Take a spoonful and drip it into the cold water. If it turns hard, it is ready.

**4** Remove the saucepan from the heat. Carefully dip each apple into the toffee. Make sure the apple is completely covered, then dip into cold water.

**5** Place the apples on the greaseproof paper and leave to cool and to set hard.

# Halloween Party Games

Because apples ripen in autumn, they have always been used for Halloween games. Here are two apple games which are good fun.

## Apple Bobbing

Fill a washing-up bowl with cold water. Place it on a table or on the floor and add plenty of apples without stems. Lean over the bowl with your hands behind your back and try to pick up an apple in your mouth. Remember to have a towel handy to wipe your face … you'll need a cloth to wipe the floor too!

## Apple Bobbing

Gotcha!
No I haven't . . .
Gotcha now!
You've gone away!
Now I've gotcha!
Oh, why bother?
I'll not eat you up today.

*Gwyn Morgan*

## Apples and Nuts

Long ago there were no sweet shops, but children still liked to eat sweet things. As they went round the houses with their masks and lanterns, they were given gifts of apples and nuts to eat. They were also given pennies.

## Bob-apple

With a metal skewer make a hole through a number of apples. (Ask an adult for help.) Cut some lengths of string and tie a knot at the end of each. Thread a string through each apple. Tie the apples by the unknotted end of the string onto a stick or a rope strung across the room, making sure the apples are not too high or too low for you to get your teeth into. The winner is the first person to finish eating an apple. Remember, you must not touch the apple with your hands – perhaps you'd better keep them behind your back! Hanging doughnuts are are also tasty party favourites.

# The Witch's Kitchen

## Which Witch?

Black witch, white witch
Which witch is which?
Can't see in the night
When it's black as pitch.
Which witch is which?
I'm in a fog.
"Too late young man –
For now you are a frog!"

## Where am I?

It's round, it's dark
It stinks a lot,
I am a little lizard
In the witch's pot.

## The Cauldron

Don't put me in the cauldron,
Don't cut me into little squares,
I'll be a good boy – promise!
For I've a mother who cares.
She'll cry if you cut me to pieces,
She'll wail all night on the bridge
That separates earthlings from heaven.
Just keep me fresh in the fridge.

*Gwyn Morgan*

# Jelly Heads

These will be a hit at your Halloween party.
Use any colour jelly (except orange, of course! Yellow doesn't work too well either). Purple and green are very effective. Ask an adult to help you cut the oranges and prepare the jelly.

## You need

- oranges
- packet of jelly
- sharp knife
- metal spoon
- bowl
- measuring jug
- wooden spoon

**1** With a sharp knife cut the top off each orange. Scoop out the flesh with a spoon. Fancy eating it? Then go ahead.

**2** Cut out spooky faces in the orange shells.

**3** Cut a thin slice off the bottom of each orange, so that it stands firmly.

**4** Make up the jelly, using a little less water than it says on the packet.

**5** Put it in the fridge to set.

**6** When the jelly has set, mash it up.

**7** Fill the orange shells with jelly.

**8** Pop the tops back on.

**9** Eat one up quickly – or there'll be none left!

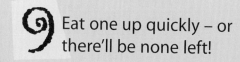

# Witches and Broomsticks

Today we use a stiff broom or a hoover to clean the floor, but in the olden days people used to use a besom – a broom made of twigs tied firmly to a wooden stick. The twigs usually came from a birch tree. Birch twigs are slender and tightly packed and are still used for sweeping leaves off the lawn.

But broomsticks had other uses too, quite apart from cleaning houses. In the old days if you were looking for a partner, you would leave a broomstick in a prominent position outside the door. Then everyone would know you wanted a husband or wife or sweetheart. 'Broomstick weddings' were held in Wales at one time, especially among the gypsies. If a couple jumped over the broomstick, it was considered a marriage ceremony.

But when we think of different uses for a broomstick, the first thing that comes to mind is a witch in a pointed hat flying through the air with her black cat clinging to the broom behind her. This is the kind of witch who wanders around on Halloween and turns up at fancy dress parties.

How do we recognise a witch? Well, probably by her long black cloak – and maybe a long crooked nose with a huge pimple at the end of it. And of course her voice! A witch always sounds old and croaky and sometimes she laughs in an evil way: 'Heh-heh-heh-heh-heh!'

What does the witch do? Well, she curses people who have offended her, of course. She stands over a huge cauldron and stirs an evil brew of toads and adders' eyes, of mouse fur and spiders. Then she chants a strange menacing spell over the mixture and waves her magic wand. One flash of lightning and one thunderclap later, some poor farmer's animal ends up lame or the wheel of his tractor is flat; a prince is changed into a frog and all the rivers are poisoned.

That is probably how we picture a witch nowadays. This image has gradually developed into a cartoon figure in our heads. But, in fact, it's very far from the truth.

It's true that witches were often associated with curses and evil spells – those were the bad witches. A good witch on the other hand could be friendly and helpful. Witches were known to have a close relationship with the earth and could understand the healing uses of herbs and leaves and the secrets of nature. They made potions to cure all sorts of illnesses, and their houses were full of leaves and roots and all kinds of things hanging up to dry. They made ointment and medicine by mixing the strangest things – that's why people started telling stories about rabbits' paws, spiders' webs and eyes of toads.

33

# Witch Hunts

At various times during the course of history, ordinary people will turn against anyone who is different and leads a secret life. Witches were persecuted, imprisoned and even killed and burnt in the old days. Often they were just lonely old women who made medicines out of plants.

Today we are once again beginning to appreciate the healthy benefits of medicines and drinks and oils made from leaves and flowers.

Who knows, perhaps if we drank the right mixture, we'd feel so nimble and healthy, we could jump on a broomstick and fly through the air!

## Busy Night for Witches

It's a busy night for witches.
That's right, it's Halloween,
That's when they will be spotted
As dusk dissolves the green.

They catch the fifty-seven bus,
And make it fly about,
No broomsticks, cats or mousy bats
At witches' first night out.

## Don't Go Out

Don't go out in the pale moonlight,
Don't go where earth meets sky,
Don't go where stars are shuddering
For there the witches fly.

## Ugly Mask

What an ugly mask you have –
Blood and pus on nose and chin,
Scars on cheeks, lumps on your forehead,
Eyes that stare . . . beware – they spin.
Fangs as sharp as any razor.
Why such ears? When did you fall?
Oh my goodness! Got to go now –
My mistake, it's not a mask at all!

## Sam

Sam's been turned into a lizard
In the eye of the silvery moon.
His mother's hoping they'll turn him back
Very, very soon.

*Gwyn Morgan*

# Weird Windows

**You will need** • A large piece of black paper • A white pencil
Scissors or a craft knife • Tissue paper of different colours • Sticky tape

**1** Draw a Halloween scene: creepy castle; pumpkin head; skull; bat; cat; ghost; witch …Keep the picture simple. Leave wide margins and make sure that every shape is joined to another shape.

**2** Cut out the background around the shapes carefully. If you are using a large piece of paper (A3 or larger) you can use scissors, but it's more difficult to cut out on a smaller sheet. Maybe you should ask an adult to cut out the shapes with a craft knife.

**3** Use the tape to stick the tissue paper to the back of your scary picture. Add lots of bright colours.

**4** Stick the front of the picture to the window.

**5** Ask an adult if you can place a table lamp behind the picture so that a strong, spooky light shines through.

Turn your house or school into Dracula's Castle or Frankenstein's Lair.

You can easily make very scary windows.

A fairy story

Emily Huws

# Morgan's Magic Music

Tap-tap-tap – on the window. Tap-tap-tap!

Morgan ap Rhys, who was snoozing in his chair by the the fire, looked round in surprise. It was a cold, miserable night of wind and rain. Who on earth had come to his lonely farmhouse on the slopes of Cader Idris in such dreadful weather?

He listened carefully for a moment, but could only hear the eerie howl of the wind around the side of the house and the pitter-patter of raindrops on the roof and on the window pane.

'I must have been dreaming,' he said to himself. Just then he heard the noise again.

Tap-tap-tap – this time on the door.

Tap-tap-tap!

Yes! – there was someone there . . .

Morgan was a kindly, friendly and welcoming man. Jumping to his feet, he called out:

'Goodness me! Come in, come in! You shouldn't be out on a night like this!'

He opened the door and in walked three travellers – at least, that's what Morgan assumed they were. They looked like travellers, but he didn't study them too closely. He never dreamt that they were three fairies – three of the Little People.

Morgan didn't know that fairies sometimes pretended to be ordinary folk and went from place to place, calling at farms and cottages to see if the people were kind and generous, welcoming and helpful.

'A hearty welcome to you!' he said. 'Come and warm yourselves by the fire after being out in such weather.'

'Thank you very much,' said the tallest and the thinnest of the three. 'We're very grateful to you for giving us shelter. I wonder if you'd be so kind as to put a little food in this bag that I'm carrying? We're starving hungry.'

'Of course!' Morgan said without a moment's hesitation. 'Wait. I'll go and fetch some bread and cheese from the pantry.'

In no time, he was back.

'Here you are,' he said. 'Three loaves that were baked this morning and some goat's cheese. Will that be enough for you?'

'Yes, indeed,' replied the shortest of the three. 'Quite enough.'

'You're welcome to it,' said Morgan. 'Help yourselves.'

The travellers put the food in their bag.

'You're very kind, Morgan ap Rhys,' said the quietest of the three. 'We're very grateful, and to show how much we appreciate your kindness, we'd like to give you a gift.'

'Oh, you needn't do that,' protested Morgan. 'I may be in need of help myself some day.'

'We are not ordinary travellers,' explained the first man.

'We can grant you any wish,' explained the second.

'What would you like?' asked the third.

'Goodness me!' exclaimed Morgan in astonishment. 'This is unexpected! A wish? Any wish? Are you really serious?'

'Of course we are! What would you like?'

Morgan thought hard for a moment. 'Well . . .' he said after a while. 'Well, I like music and I've been longing for a harp for years and years. Please could I have a harp?'

Morgan watched the three of them whisper to each other. 'I don't want to cause you any trouble,' he added worriedly.

'It's no trouble at all,' said the fairies. 'Yes, you may have a harp. As long as you close your eyes and don't peep till you hear the door close behind us. Do you promise?'

'Yes,' agreed Morgan in amazement.

He closed his eyes. He heard the door creak open. He felt a sharp breeze on the back of his neck. He heard the door close. He opened his eyes.

There in front of him stood a wonderful golden harp. He was not a very good harpist, so he touched the strings very gingerly, but this was a magic fairy harp, which could play without much help from him.

The next morning, Morgan's wife returned. She had been visiting neighbours and had stayed the night. Several of them had come back with her for a cup of tea and a chat. They were thrilled when they saw the harp.

'Would you like to hear me play it?' asked Morgan.

'Yes, Morgan. Yes, we would,' said everyone.

The lively music made everyone's toes tingle. It made them immediately get up and start dancing. At top speed they whirled around the room – they couldn't help themselves. Morgan's fingers flashed across the strings, the music got faster and faster and the dancers dance-dance-danced till they were fit to drop. While the harp played they could not stop dancing. They had to keep at it.

'Stop, Morgan!' begged his wife. 'I've a terrible stitch in my side.'

But Morgan only laughed.

'Our feet are hurting, Morgan bach!' called some of the neighbours.

But Morgan laughed and went on playing the harp.

Faster than the wind, wilder than a stormy sea, the music swept on and on and the dancers leapt higher and higher.

Then at last Morgan realised that they were all looking pale and weak and very tired, so he stopped playing the harp. But he kept on laughing, which annoyed his guests. They didn't think it was at all funny.

Soon news of the astonishing harp spread through the whole area. Morgan was delighted with the wonderful music, but no one else had a good word to say for the harp. They hated it, because everyone who heard the music had no choice – they had to dance!

Many had suffered dreadfully. Some people slept for a whole week after dancing all night to the music of Morgan's harp. Morgan was not in the least bit popular.

His wife begged him to give it up. His friends advised him kindly to play less often. Others suggested he should find a lonely spot where no one would be able hear him. But Morgan turned a deaf ear. He refused to listen to anyone. He went on playing his harp.

Then, after a terrible night when Morgan had played non-stop and everyone was in a bad way, the harp disappeared. When Morgan woke up in the morning, there was no sign of it.

'Have you seen my harp anywhere?' he asked his neighbours in a panic.

They all shook their heads and gave sighs of relief.

'We don't know anything!' they said. 'We didn't see anything. We didn't hear anything either.'

But his wife, who had gone out at daybreak to milk the goats, had glimpsed three strangers, travellers maybe, lurking around the house. Morgan had misused the fairies' gift, and so the Little People had decided to be kind to the folk who lived around Cader Idris. They had taken the magic harp away from him.

His friends and neighbours were delighted; they never wanted to set eyes on a harp again, but poor Morgan's heart was breaking.

For the rest of his life, every cold miserable night of wind and rain when he was in the house on his own, he would turn his head and listen hard, hoping to hear:

Tap-tap-tap – on the window.

Tap-tap-tap!

Then, Tap-tap-tap – on the door.

Tap-tap-tap!

Just like that.

And again.

But from that day on the only things he heard were the eerie howl of the wind around the side of the house and the pitter-patter of raindrops on the roof and on the windowpane.

# Finding Your True Love

Long ago, young men and women looked forward to Halloween. At Halloween they might be able to discover the identity of their true love.

Many thought the face of a future husband or wife would appear in the mirror, if they combed their hair while eating an apple at midnight on Halloween.

In the Towy valley, to find out who they were going to marry, they would peel an apple very carefully in one long strip (the spell didn't work if the strip broke). The young people would take the apple peel and whirl it three times around their heads, chanting:

*Peel the apple at Halloween,*
*Remember to keep the peel in one piece,*
*Apple peel, apple peel,*
*Tell me my fortune at Halloween.*

Then they would drop the peel behind them. If the peel formed the shape of a letter, that would be the initial of the person who they would marry.

In Pembrokeshire they would use a swede. The swede would be washed and peeled. Then it would be hung behind the kitchen door, and the peel would be buried in the garden. The girl who had peeled the swede was certain to marry a man with the same name as the first man to walk in through the kitchen door.

Another method was to make a cake and drop a ring, a thimble and a coin into the mixture. Whoever ended up with the coin would be rich. The person who had the ring would soon be married. But the poor person who found the thimble would not ever marry.

In the county of Caernarfon the girls would use a snail.

> *Look for a snail*
> *Put it under a bowl*
> *And into the house you go.*
> *Leave overnight,*
> *Then peek at its trail.*
> *Is there a letter? If so,*
> *You'll marry a man*
> *Whose initial it is.*
> *'O' for Owen. For Ifan an 'I'.*
> *That's how we maids*
> *Find our sweethearts, you see.*
> *We'll marry these men by and by.*
>
> *But if that old snail hasn't left you a trail,*
> *That's a very bad omen, I'm told.*
> *You will not marry with Tom, Dick or Harry*
> *For the love that you had has grown cold.*

There was a special spell to find out how your true love earned his or her living. An egg would be broken over a bowl of water. The white of the egg would be separated from the yolk and dropped into the water. The shape formed by the white of the egg would give you the answer. If it stood up in peaks, it meant that the person had to work in town, but if it sank to the bottom in lumps, it meant your true love was a farmer.

Nine was an important number in love spells at Halloween. In Montgomeryshire young people would often make Nine Type Mash on Halloween. Nine Type Mash was a stew of potatoes, carrots, turnips, peas, parsnips, leeks, pepper, salt and milk. A wedding ring would be hidden in the mash and whoever found the ring on his plate would soon marry.

Another custom was to walk around the church nine times in the hope of meeting your true love coming towards you on the ninth lap.

In Ceredigion a young man would walk around his home nine times with a glove in his hand and ask, 'Here is a glove, where is the hand?' Then his sweetheart would appear and place her hand in the glove.

Sometimes the young man would carry a shoe and would ask: 'Here is a shoe, where is the foot?'

In the county of Caernarfon a young person would throw a ball of wool out of the window, wait for the sweetheart to catch it and say:

> *I'm the thrower.*
> *Whoever catches it,*
> *Come here!*

Some couples would plant seeds in the garden, leeks for example, and would call out:

> *Whoever wants to live with me*
> *Come and take a rake with me.*

Others would throw hemp seeds over their shoulders and call out:

> *Here I am sowing hemp seeds.*
> *If you love me, come and gather them.*

# Beware

Beware, my little darling,
Those goblins, blood they sup,
And in a twinkling of an eye
They'll have you gobbled up.
The trees have turned their colour
From golden into rust,
'Twill be the witching hour
When bones are ground to dust.

# Unlike Elephants

Witches, unlike elephants
Live upside down in caves,
Fly about on Halloween,
And have some wicked raves.
They'll turn you into concrete slabs,
Perhaps into a chimp:
Oops, one's crashed into a taxicab
That's why she has a limp.

# Please Don't ...

Please don't turn me into a frog,
Into a lizard, newt or dog;
Please don't turn me into a pig,
Into a cat, a mouse or a fig.
Turn me into a handsome king,
Let me wear a golden ring,
Please, sweet witch, on Halloween
Let me wed a pretty queen.

# My Dad Says ...

That witches zoom on brooms with cats,
And can turn you into a lizard;
They weave their spells in cauldrons black –
He knows, 'cause he's a wizard.

*Gwyn Morgan*

Myrddin ap Dafydd

# The Black Lady of Cardiff

In Glamorgan, female ghosts are called 'Ladi' or 'Lady', and they're usually distinguished by their colour. There are many 'White Ladies' in the area. Between Melingriffith and Tongwynlais there is a well which is known as 'White Lady's Well', because the ghost of a woman in white has been seen there.

At one time a 'Grey Lady' used to haunt the centre of Cardiff. She wore a grey cloak and would be seen walking down Queen Street, crossing the bridge over the river Taff, and waving her hand at someone – and then she would disappear.

But the Black Lady was always seen near the harbour. Cardiff was only a small village at the time. The Black Lady, dressed in black, would walk back and forth along the quay, wandering this way and that as if she was searching for something.

Many sailors saw the Black Lady but not one was brave enough to go to her and ask what was wrong. Sometimes she would hold out her hands to them and walk towards the boats at the water's edge, but she would disappear if no one was willing to walk with her. If a sailor spoke to her she could answer, but she was mute unless someone spoke first.

One evening, a ship's captain dared to approach the Black Lady.

'Can I help you?' he asked. As he was the one who had spoken first, she was able to answer him.

'Take me to the mouth of the river Ely,' said the Black Lady. 'If you are brave enough to help me, you will be richly rewarded.'

The captain agreed to take her and stepped into his rowing boat. The lady followed and sat in the stern. The captain began to row into the deep waters of the river and as he manoeuvered his boat through the current, it became more and more difficult to pull on the oars. The boat's load seemed to be getting heavier and heavier with every passing second.

Soon the rowing boat was lying low in the water and they were far from shore. The captain began to worry that the boat would sink beneath such a heavy weight. He was about to say so, when the Black Lady interrupted his thoughts.

'That's it,' she said. 'We've come far enough. Now head for the bank.'

The captain rowed gratefully towards land and dragged the boat onto the shingle. The Black Lady had already begun to walk away through the woods that grew on the riverbank. The captain followed her. After walking for some distance through the woods, they came to an enormous stone.

'I want you to lift this stone,' said the Black Lady.

The stone was very heavy and the captain was afraid that he would never be able to shift it, but he found the strength from somewhere and after much groaning and sweating, he managed at last to lift the stone and roll it to one side. What a sight met his eyes! In the hole where the stone had lain lay a crock full of gold.

'I have been trying to reach this treasure for many a long year,' said the Black Lady. 'Until tonight no one was brave enough to assist me. As a reward for your help, Captain, the gold is now yours.'

With that the Black Lady disappeared. The captain looked down in astonishment at the crock of gold. Gradually it dawned on him that he would never be short of money for the rest of his days. Not only that, but he and his family were immensely rich! He slipped a handful of gold into his pocket and rolled the stone back into place over the crock.

Many times after that, he rowed back to the mouth of the river Ely and lifted the stone in the woods. He used the gold wisely to buy a ship for himself and employed a captain and crew to sail it, so that he didn't have to leave his family so often. He bought a fine house in Cardiff and became a very rich man.

A short while before he died he told the secret to his children – the secret of the Black Lady's treasure. And they in turn told this story to me.

# Ghostly Grub

Every Halloween the witches have a party, and the party food is absolutely disgusting! Pretend to your friends that the food in your party is going to be just as foul.

All these recipes sound and look horrible and very yucky. But don't be fooled. They are all delicious! If you're going to try them out, ask an adult for help. **Do not use an oven on your own.**

## Revolting Rolls

**Use**

- Bread rolls
- Long, green beans or onion stalks to make legs
- Pieces of carrot, cucumber, tomatoes, grapes or radish for eyes
- A row of sweet corn for teeth
- Pieces of ham/salami for tongues that hang out
- Use your imagination . . .

## Perilous Pizzas

Use vegetables to make faces (ugly ones, of course!) on your pizzas.

# Crazy Cakes

**To make 20 cakes you need**

- 125g softened butter or margarine
- 125g white caster sugar
- 125g self-raising flour
- 1 teaspoon baking powder
- 2 large eggs
- 1 teaspoon vanilla essence
- a mixing bowl
- wooden and metal spoons
- 20 paper cake cases
- a bun tin

**To decorate**

- 100g icing sugar
- 1 tablespoon water (or orange/lemon juice)
- pieces of liquorice
- cherry halves
- tubes of writing icing
- jelly sweets or any sweets with interesting shapes

**1** Put all the ingredients in a bowl and beat well with a wooden spoon until soft. Better still, use a food mixer. Ask an adult for help.

**2** Divide the mixture among the paper cases (about a teaspoonful in each).

**3** Bake in the oven for 18-20 minutes (190°C/375°F/Gas Mark 5). Leave them to cool completely before beginning to decorate. You can make eyeballs, a spider in a web and a lot of other disgusting things.

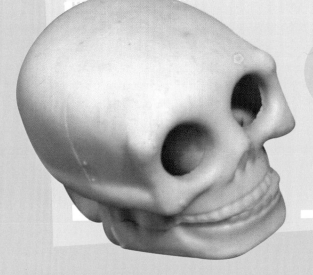

Siân Lewis

# The Magic Ointment

It was the first night of spring and the full moon shone brightly on Garth Dorwen farm. In the field near the house sat a young woman with the moonlight dancing on her yellow hair. Her name was Eilian. She was the maid at Garth Dorwen and she was busy at her spinning wheel.

In the farmhouse kitchen Abel and Mali Prydderch were sitting contentedly in front of the fire.

'Oh Abel,' said Mali to her husband. 'We're so lucky to have a maid like Eilian.'

'I couldn't agree with you more,' said Abel. 'Hiring Eilian at the Halloween Fair was the best thing we ever did.'

There was no maid like her. Eilian worked hard in the house all day long and at nightfall she went out to the field to spin by the light of the moon.

'Look, it's ten o'clock and she's still hard at work,' said Mali. 'I'll go and call her now. It's time she came inside.'

Abel nodded wisely and watched his wife open the back door.

'Eilian!' called Mali. 'Eilian!'

There was no reply.

'Eilian!' she called again.

Still there was no reply.

Abel jumped to his feet and headed across the farmyard with his wife at his heels. When they reached the field gate, they both turned pale. Eilian's spinning wheel lay turning on the grass, but where was Eilian? There was no sign of her. Their maid had disappeared.

For many long months Abel and Mali searched for Eilian. They questioned all their neighbours, but no one had news of her.

Then one dark night there came a knock at the door of Garth Dorwen. Carefully Mali lifted the latch and peeped out.

From the shadows a voice spoke. 'Are you Mali Prydderch?'

'Yes,' she replied.

Abel hurried to the door with a lantern. By its light they saw a fine gentleman on a sleek black horse. The gentleman was dressed all in black.

'My wife is about to have a baby,' said the gentleman to Mali. 'Will you come and help her?'

'Of course I will,' said Mali, reaching for her cloak. She was well used to bringing babies into the world.

The gentleman reached down from the saddle, swung her up behind him and off raced the horse.

As soon as she'd got her breath back, Mali peeped over the stranger's shoulder. To her surprise they were galloping across a lonely heath towards a hill called Bryn y Pibion.

She was even more surprised when the horse entered a huge cavern in the side of the hill. At the far end of the cavern stood a magnificent palace of gold and silver, with bright lights flooding from its many windows.

The horse came to a halt in front of the open door. The gentleman dismounted, lifted Mali from the saddle and led the way through halls and passageways to the finest room Mali had ever seen. There, beside a roaring fire, lay a young woman on a bed spread with silken sheets.

'Call me when the baby is born,' said the gentleman, turning smartly on his heel and leaving the room.

'I will,' Mali promised.

Within half an hour Mali was wrapping the new-born baby in a lace robe. She called the father, who returned at once bearing a pot of ointment.

'I'd like you to do me one more favour,' he said. 'Rub this ointment over the baby's eyes, but make very sure that it doesn't touch your own. If you do as you're told, I shall take you home and give you a purse full of gold.'

The gentleman went away again and Mali settled down by the fire with the baby on her knee. Carefully she dipped her finger into the ointment and smeared it over the baby's right eye. She smeared more ointment over his left eye. All was well till a small spark jumped from the fire and landed on Mali's cheek. Without thinking, she flicked it away and, as she did so, she accidentally touched her left eye with the greasy finger.

In a moment the lights dimmed.

The fire died in the grate.

The fine palace disappeared.

On Mali's knee nestled a ragged little baby. His mother lay on a bed of straw on the cave floor with the sputtering light of a candle reflected on her yellow hair.

With a gasp Mali recognised the yellow hair. 'Eilian!' she cried.

'Mistress!' Eilian sat up in dismay.

'What are you doing here, Eilian?' said Mali, rushing over to her.

'The fairies took me away,' said the maid.

'Then come home with me this minute!' pleaded Mali.

'I can never go home,' said Eilian, taking the baby in her arms. 'And if my husband knows you've recognised me, you'll never go home either. Sh!' They could hear footsteps. Eilian pulled Mali towards her and whispered in her ear. 'Don't say a word, Mistress. Please don't, or you'll never see Mr Prydderch again!'

The dark shadow of Eilian's husband appeared at the cave entrance.

'Ready?' he said to Mali.

A quarter of an hour later Mali was back safely in the kitchen of Garth Dorwen with a purse full of gold in her hand.

With the gold Abel and Mali went to the Halloween Fair in Caernarfon to hire another maid. After they'd struck a bargain with a cheerful, rosy-cheeked girl, they both went their separate ways.

Mali was busy admiring some dinner plates, when she noticed a thief at the next stall. The man was taking trinkets from under the stall-keeper's nose and stuffing them into the pocket of his black coat.

'How dare he!' said Mali. She strode towards him shouting, 'Hey! Stop…!'

The words died on her lips, for the man who turned towards her was Eilian's husband.

'Oh, hello,' babbled Mali. 'How are Eilian and the baby?'

A harsh smile spread over the man's face. 'So you can see me, Mali Prydderch,' he hissed. 'Can you see me with both eyes?'

Mali closed one eye, then the other. 'No, I can only see you with this one,' she said, pointing at her left eye where she'd rubbed the ointment.

At once the man blew into the left eye and blinded it.

And that was the last time Mali ever saw the Fairies.

# Diabolical Drinks

## Swallowing, slurping and sipping in style

Monstrous mouthfuls! Spooky sips! Ghastly gulps!
It looks as if they're all here. But try one and see.
You may be pleasantly surprised – thank goodness!

### You need

- Tall glasses
- Drinking straws
- A plastic bag and rolling pin for crushing the ice
- Plastic decorations
- Coloured ice cubes
- Orange, tomato and cranberry juice
- Twiglets
- Ice cream
- Lemonade
- Coke
- Frozen chocolate buttons
- Marshmallows

### How to make and mash ice

Add a few drops of green food colouring to a jug of water, pour into an ice cube tray and leave in the freezer overnight – simple but effective. You could put some of the cubes in a plastic bag, tie the top and mash them with a rolling pin.

### 1 Blood 'n Bones

Pour the tomato juice into a glass. Place Twiglets and marsh-mallows around the mouth of the glass. Drink quickly before the Twiglets go mushy!

### 2 Chilly Stripes

Mash cubes of plain ice, green ice, orange and cranberry juice ice separately. Place one layer on top of another in a glass.

### 3 Freaky Fizz

Put a dollop of ice cream into a glass of coke and stand back!

### 4 Galloping Green

Throw some green ice cubes into lemonade and watch the green whirl around.

### 5 Button Bob

Drop the frozen chocolate buttons into the lemonade and watch them bob around.

# Spooky Stories

## The Ghost Train

Ghost stories go down well at a party. Before the big night, try and think of a brilliant ghost tale with which to scare your friends. Write it down, and collect an assortment of things that your friends can hear and touch while you tell the story. Remember to practise ways of making your story really scary. Then, on the night, ask a volunteer to sit on a chair with a blindfold around his/her eyes. Then tell a story that goes something like this:

One dark night, a long time ago, a train was travelling across Dead Man's Bog (*make the noise of a train rattling over the track*). It was very quiet and all the passengers were asleep, when suddenly – (*blow a whistle or recorder*) – the driver sounded his whistle. A huge shape was standing on the track. It was an enormous dog, larger than a bull. It refused to move. The driver could not stop (*loud crash – drop spoons into an empty biscuit tin*). The train crashed into the monster and everyone was hurled into the bog. They disappeared under the mud, without any chance of escape.

One Halloween an old witch began to poke around in the bog. She found lots of weird and wonderful things. "Heh heh heh!' she cackled. "This is just the thing for (*the name of the person who's sitting in the chair*)! Hold out your hand!"

Here is the monster's ear (*a juicy apricot or peach from a tin*).

Here are his huge eyes (*grapes*).

Here is his long tongue (*a banana*).

Here is his long tail (*strands of wet wool*).

Once you get going, you'll think up all sorts of spooky ideas …

# Dracula and his Friends: A Drama

For some Halloween fun, how about acting out a devilish drama-a-a-ah!? Sights and sounds are important in a drama, so dig out some scary props – a cloak, a bat, a huge spider, a witch's hat. Remember to practise. To create the right atmosphere on the night, open the door and hang a white sheet across the opening. Make sure there's a light behind it. While telling your story, hang or place shapes behind the sheet to make scary shadows, and remember to use plenty of spooky sounds as well.

One moonlit night a boy was walking past an old church. He heard the rustle of leaves in the tree above his head (*move your hands inside a noisy plastic bag*). A man in a black cloak landed on the ground next to him. "Dracula needs a boy's blood for supper!" he screeched.

The boy ran for his life to the churchyard . . .

# Party Tricks

You must have fun at a party, and good games are always fun. Remember to reward everyone who takes part – only the bravest will want to!

## Slime Splosh

In a bucket, mix flour and water to make a gooey mess. The mixture must be so thick that no one can see what's in it. Put lots of tiny things in the slime. Will your friends be brave enough to dip their hands inside and fish them out?

## Fearless Fingers

You'll need them to play this ghastly game!

The idea is to make people dip their fingers into boxes full of disgusting things they can't see. YUCK!

In the top of a box cut a hole that is large enough for your hand. Inside place a plate or bowl full of disgusting things . . . wet spaghetti worms, or grape eyes.

If you cut away one side of the box, you'll be able to check if the person really has got fearless fingers!

A ghost story

Myrddin ap Dafydd

# Trouble at the Inn

In the village of Cwm near the Flintshire coast in north-east Wales there is an interesting old pub called the Blue Lion. Four hundred years ago, the building was part of a farm.

In those days, the inn and the farm were run by a man called Siôn Harri, along with his father and brother. But Siôn quarrelled with the other two. The quarrel led to a fight in which poor Siôn was killed.

No one in the area knew that anything was wrong. The next day, the father and son spread a rumour that Siôn Harri had suddenly decided to emigrate to America and had left without warning. At first everyone believed them, but people became suspicious when some of the customers at the inn saw the ghost of Siôn Harri wandering through the rooms.

The village churchyard is directly behind the Blue Lion and some two hundred years later, the villagers went to tidy it up. They lifted fallen gravestones and cleared some of the old soil. As they did so, they came across a skeleton that had been buried on top of a coffin. This meant that it had been buried in a hurry and in suspicious circumstances. The

discovery was at once linked to the story of Siôn Harri's ghost, especially as a ghost was still haunting the inn.

Although the body had been discovered, the ghost remained. People often heard it walking along the corridors, but when they went to look, there was never anyone there. Sometimes the landlady would see it – it would stand and watch her for a while, and then it would duck as if it were walking under the low beam that had once been part of the doorway.

Siôn's ghost made its presence felt in many other ways too. In 1969 the landlord kept a small zoo behind the pub, which consisted of a monkey, several snakes and an alligator. One morning, every cage had been opened and all the animals set free! He managed to find them all and put them back in their cages, but the same thing happened the following night.

He suspected it was the work of an animal rights group, so he spread sand on the floor in order to capture the footprints of the vandals. That night the animals escaped for the third time – but no human footprints were left in the sand. This happened five times in all, although strong locks and chains had been placed on each door.

Strange things still happen there. Things fall off the walls without warning, especially if they are metal objects, such as horse brasses. There is a room in the pub which is very, very cold – even at the height of summer – and the owners' dog will never set foot there.

The local people are certain of one thing – if Siôn Harri did go to America, he did not take his ghost with him!

# Dracula's Cake

## What to do

1. Heat the oven to 190°C/375°F/Gas 5.
2. Cream together the butter and sugar with the wooden spoon.
3. Beat in each egg, adding a little flour as you go.
4. Fold in the rest of the flour with a metal spoon.
5. Divide the mixture in two. Leave one half plain and add cocoa powder to the other.
6. Put alternate spoonfuls of the two mixtures into the baking tin.
7. To create a marbled effect, gently swirl with a knife.
8. Bake for about 25 minutes till the cake looks spongy on top.
9. Roll out the icing.
10. Remove the cake from the oven and leave to cool on the rack.
11. Cut the cake in half, and cut out three semicircles from the straight edge of each half. These are the bat wings.
12. Make a bat's head from the solid icing and place it between the two wings.
13. Cover with runny icing and use the liquorice to make wing lines.

## You will need

- 2 mixing bowls
- A wooden spoon
- A 20cm/8" round cake tin
- A knife
- A cooling rack
- A metal spoon

## Ingredients

- 175g butter/margarine
- 175g sugar
- 3 eggs
- 175g self-raising flour
- 2 tablespoons cocoa powder
- Ready-made black roll-out icing
- Black runny icing
- Liquorice

# Green Martian Cake

## You will need

- A pudding bowl
- A wooden spoon
- A knife
- A cooling rack

## Ingredients

- 125g softened margarine
- 125g caster sugar
- 2 eggs
- 125g self-raising flour
- 100g green glacé icing
- Liquorice and sweets

## What to do

1 Heat the oven to 190°C/375°F/Gas 5.
2 Grease the bowl well.
3 Cream the sugar and margarine together.
4 Add beaten eggs.
5 Fold in the flour.
6 Bake for about 20 minutes until spongy.
7 Remove the cake from the oven and leave to cool on the rack.
8 Cover with the green icing and decorate with liquorice and sweets as shown in the picture.

# Mouse Munches

## You will need

- Plastic gloves to protect your hands from the black colouring

## Ingredients

- Roll-out icing
- Black food colouring
- Liquorice
- Pine nuts

## What to do

Knead the icing and colouring to make mouse shapes. Add liquorice tails and pine nut ears.

# The Empty Grave in Conwy

The old graveyard in the middle of Conwy is a quiet spot away from the noise and bustle of the surrounding streets. There you will find something very unusual – an empty grave. This is the story.

When the bridges were built across the river Conwy and the railway reached the town, visitors flocked to Conwy in summer to spend a week or two in the hotels. These were, of course, very rich families who came to enjoy the wonderful scenery and were willing to spend a lot of money. Soon more hotels were built and more and more workers were needed to wait upon the important visitors. In those days, a hotel maid was very well paid compared to a farm maid or a fisherwoman.

One summer, a young girl from Anglesey came to work in one of the hotels. She had heard about the money that could be made there and was willing to work hard so she would have a good sum to take back home with her at the end of the summer.

Unfortunately, before very long, the adventure turned sour. Shortly after she started work at the hotel she began to miss her home and her little village back in Anglesey. She could not eat, and soon she became pitifully thin. Her face grew pale and there were black shadows around her eyes.

'When I die,' she said to some of the other workers in the hotel, 'make sure that I am not buried in Conwy. I want my body to be taken back to my little village in Anglesey.'

Her fellow workers laughed.

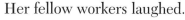

'Don't talk such nonsense!' they said. 'You're tired, that's all. You're just not used to hard work!' They were too young and too busy to listen to the solemn request of the Anglesey girl.

Then one day in the middle of the holiday season, the little maid died. The hotel was extremely busy so they had to arrange her funeral quickly – and she was buried in the graveyard in the middle of town.

 After that, everything seemed to go wrong in the hotel. When the head waiter walked into the dining room on the night of the funeral, he tripped and spilled the contents of his heavily-laden tray all over some of the visitors. A maid was washing a floor in the hotel. She turned away from her bucket for a moment and when she turned back the bucket had disappeared. The lamps would not light, even though they were full of oil. The hot water jugs cracked and broke . . .

The visitors started complaining. The hotel began to get a bad reputation. The owner was almost at the end of his tether . . .

Then one of the kitchen maids remembered the request of the Anglesey maid. She said that the girl had wanted her body to be taken home to her native village.

At once arrangements were made to remove her body from Conwy churchyard, and she was laid to rest in a grave on the banks of the Menai Strait, in the place that had been so close to her heart. In the hotel everything returned to normal and from then on the servants were able to carry out their duties without disturbance.

But the empty grave by the church is still there to remind us of the sad young maid who died of homesickness.

# Halloween throughout the World

Throughout the world people hold festivals and parties at the end of October or the beginning of November to celebrate Halloween (31 October), All Saints' Day (1 November) and All Souls' Day (2 November). It's astonishing how similar many of these celebrations are.

# In the Churchyard

Some people still believe that the ghosts of the dead come back to visit their families, and so they gather at the graves and perform certain ceremonies to remember their loved ones and celebrate their lives. At the graves of their relatives, the people of Mexico have picnics of bread and sweets shaped like coffins, skeletons or skull-and-crossbones. In Portugal the picnickers take sugar cakes containing cinnamon and spices to the graveyard, and also wine and chestnuts.

## Festive Feasts

Italians make bean-shaped cakes which they call 'The Beans of the Dead'. The Spanish, in their celebrations, eat a special pastry called 'Bones of the Blessed'.